TREASURY OF LIT

MW01382780

Grammar Practice
TEACHER'S EDITION

Grade 2

Printed in the United States of America

ISBN 0-15-305366-6

6 7 8 9 10   073   97 96

HARCOURT BRACE & COMPANY
ORLANDO · ATLANTA · AUSTIN · BOSTON · SAN FRANCISCO · CHICAGO · DALLAS · NEW YORK ·
TORONTO · LONDON

To the Teacher

This *Grammar Practice* book contains practice exercises for each Grammar Minilesson in SIDEWALKS SING and ALL KINDS OF FRIENDS. In addition, it contains a section that focuses on improving students' proofreading skills.

PROOFREADING MAKES PERFECT consists of sequenced exercises that help students learn to proofread more effectively for errors in punctuation, capitalization, spelling, and usage.

- In the first set of exercises for each part, the errors are identified.
- In each succeeding set of exercises, students are given fewer clues to the errors.
- Finally, students proofread sentences to find errors for which no clues are given.

You may wish to have students complete **PROOFREADING MAKES PERFECT** independently, in pairs, or in cooperative groups, discussing the corrections after students finish each section. At any time during the year, students may return to **PROOFREADING MAKES PERFECT** to refresh their proofreading skills.

Contents

PROOFREADING YOUR OWN WRITING

Name _____

You know it's important to write correctly. When you do, your writing is easier to understand.

A way to check your writing is to proofread it. When you proofread, you make sure that everything is correct. The activities on these pages will help you learn to proofread.

PART 1: Capital Letters and End Marks

Step 1.

The mistakes in these sentences have been pointed out for you. Write the sentences correctly.

    capital
    letters   period

1. on tuesday the elephant had a party __

    On Tuesday the elephant had a party. _____

    capital   exclamation
    letter   point

2. how hot the day was __

    How hot the day was! _____

    capital   capital
    letter   letter   period

3. So rocky and ellen wore their swimsuits __

    So Rocky and Ellen wore their swimsuits. _____

Harcourt Brace School Publishers

Step 2.

Proofread the sentences for capital letters and end marks. Underline the mistakes. Then write the sentences correctly.

YOU'RE INVITED!

1. my birthday is on friday

   My birthday is on Friday.

2. the date is march 12

   The date is March 12.

3. can you come to my party

   Can you come to my party?

4. a clown named happy will be there

   A clown named Happy will be there.

5. what fun we will have

   What fun we will have!

Name _____

PART 2: Spelling

Step 1.
Read the sentences. The words that are underlined are not spelled correctly. Write the correct spelling.

1. Let's <u>pla</u> ball.

   play _____

2. I'm going to <u>hitt</u> the ball really hard.

   hit _____

3. I <u>jist</u> got a <u>hom</u> run!

   just, home _____

4. I <u>licke</u> this <u>gam</u> so much!

   like, game _____

Step 2.
Find the number of mistakes given for each sentence. Write each sentence correctly.

Find two mistakes.

1. Do Salty an Bo hav their mitts?

   Do Salty and Bo have their mitts?

Find two mistakes.

2. "Let's go sea the game," sed Lumpy.

   "Let's go see the game," said Lumpy.

Find three mistakes.

3. Hep Bo when hee is upp at bat.

   Help Bo when he is up at bat.

Step 3.
Now proofread for spelling mistakes with no clues.
Write each sentence correctly.

4. I bett Salty's dade came to see us plae.

   I bet Salty's dad came to see us play.

5. Last time hee set with teh team.

   Last time he sat with the team.

6. Com and gifv us a batting lesson know.

   Come and give us a batting lesson now.

Name _____

PART 3: Word Use

Step 1.

Look at each picture. Write <u>is</u>, <u>am</u>, or <u>are</u> in the sentence under the picture.

1. I _____**am**_____ a toy pony.

2. My spots _____**are**_____ black.

3. Our barn _____**is**_____ big.

4. Two ponies _____**are**_____ ready.

Step 2.

Can you correct the underlined mistakes?
Write the sentences correctly.

5. Erica and Matty <u>has</u> toy ponies.

   Erica and Matty have toy ponies.

6. One pony <u>are</u> white with black spots.

   One pony is white with black spots.

7. The girls <u>is</u> happy with their game.

   The girls are happy with their game.

8. Matty's pony <u>come</u> into the barn.

   Matty's pony comes into the barn.

Step 3.

Now proofread with no clues.
Write each sentence correctly.

9. This horse do work for farmers.

   This horse does work for farmers.

10. Now men comes to feed him.

    Now men come to feed him.

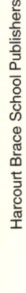

Name

Proofreading is important. You have practiced proofreading for capital letters and end marks, for spelling, and for correct verbs. When these things are correct, your writing is easier to read and understand. Now you can practice proofreading for all these kinds of mistakes, just as you do with your own writing.

PART 4: Wrap-Up

Step 1.

Look at the signs in this picture. Four signs have mistakes. Write the words correctly on the lines below the picture.

1. **Clark Street**

2. **River Road**

3. **Mr. Smith's Books**

4. **ride**

Step 2.

Proofread the sentences. The mistakes have been underlined. Write the sentences correctly.

5. my grandma en grandpa comes today

My grandma and grandpa come today.

6. they drives here every april fool's day

They drive here every April Fool's Day.

7. when they come, i giv them a big hug.

When they come, I give them a big hug.

8. my grandpa's real name is mr kidd

My grandpa's real name is Mr. Kidd.

9. Do he and mrs kidd bring their pets

Do he and Mrs. Kidd bring their pets?

10. yes, they comes with winger and goldie

Yes, they come with Winger and Goldie.

Name

Hello!

Step 3.
Now proofread with no clues.
Write the sentences correctly.

11. on tuesday Grandpa play tricks

On Tuesday Grandpa plays tricks.

12. what wile he doo

What will he do?

13. wow, you won't believe thes

Wow, you won't believe this!

14. he and Grandma likes to hide

He and Grandma like to hide.

15. they takes winger wid them

They take Winger with them.

16. one time i wint by their hiding place

One time I went by their hiding place.

17. suddenly winger talked to me

Suddenly Winger talked to me.

SENTENCES

Name _____

A **sentence** is a group of words that tells a complete thought. Every sentence begins with a capital letter and ends with a special mark.

A. Read each group of words. Circle <u>yes</u> if the words make a sentence. Circle <u>no</u> if the words do not make a sentence. The first one has been done for you.

1. My name is Eeky.   (yes)   no

2. live in the wall   yes   (no)

3. I eat cheese.   (yes)   no

4. Smokey the cat   yes   (no)

5. chases me   yes   (no)

6. I run fast.   (yes)   no

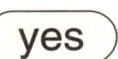

B. Read each set of words. Write the group of words that is a sentence. The first one has been done for you.

1. I visit my friends.   Fuzzy and Curly

   I visit my friends.

2. have fun   We eat cookies.

   We eat cookies.

3. Fuzzy and Curly dance.   the music

   Fuzzy and Curly dance.

4. play the banjo   We sing songs.

   We sing songs.

Activity Corner ▽▲▽▲▽▲▽▲▽▲▽▲▽

Write two funny sentences about Eeky and his friends.

_____

_____

_____

_____

_____

Name _____

A sentence has a **naming part** that names who or what the sentence is about.

A. Read each sentence. Write the naming part. The first one has been done for you.

1. A spaceship lands on Earth.

   A spaceship _____

2. The windows are round.

   The windows _____

3. Zibby is small.

   Zibby _____

4. Zona is tall.

   Zona _____

5. The space people live on Bluna.

   The space people _____

6. Their home is far away.

   Their home _____

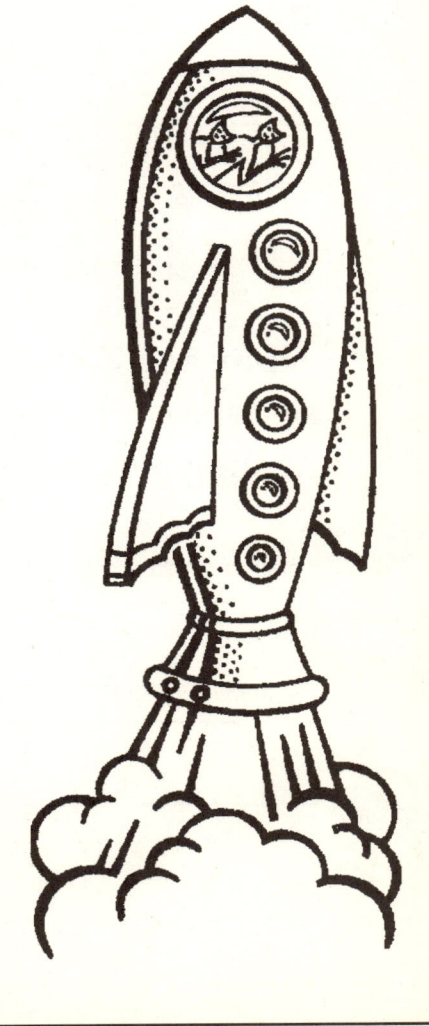

B. Write each sentence. Circle the naming part. The first one has been done for you.

1. Zibby finds rocks.

   (Zibby) finds rocks.

2. The bag is full.

   (The bag) is full.

3. Zona picks flowers.

   (Zona) picks flowers.

Activity Corner

Zibby and Zona collect things from Earth. Write three sentences about things they might collect. Circle the naming part in each sentence.

_____

_____

_____

_____

Name _____

Sometimes the naming parts of two sentences can be joined. The word <u>and</u> is used to join the naming parts to make one sentence.

A. Join the naming parts of the two sentences to make one sentence. The first one has been done for you.

1. Giraffe marched in the parade. Hippo marched in the parade.

   Giraffe and Hippo marched in the parade.

   _____

2. Bear danced a silly dance. Monkey danced a silly dance.

   Bear and Monkey danced a silly dance.

   _____

3. Elephants carried flowers. Horses carried flowers.

   Elephants and horses carried flowers.

B. Join each pair of sentences. Write new sentences. Use the word and. The first one has been done for you.

1. Lion skated to a song. Tiger skated to a song.

   Lion and Tiger skated to a song.

2. The chimps rode bikes. The dogs rode bikes.

   The chimps and the dogs rode bikes.

3. Rat played the flute. Mole played the flute.

   Rat and Mole played the flute.

Activity Corner ▼▲▼▲▼▲▼▲▼▲▼▲▼

There are two more animals in the parade. They are jumping down the street. Give them names and draw pictures of them on a separate sheet of paper. Write a sentence about each animal. Then join the naming parts by using the word and.

_____

_____

_____

_____

Name

A sentence has a **telling part** that tells what someone or something <u>is</u> or <u>does</u>.

A. Read each sentence. Write the telling part. The first one has been done for you.

1. Rooty ran across the field.

   ran across the field

2. She was late for dinner.

   was late for dinner

3. Doogie was hungry.

   was hungry

4. He jumped up and down.

   jumped up and down

5. Rooty and Rusty sat at the table.

   sat at the table

B. Look at each picture. Choose the correct telling part. Write it in the sentence.

1. Rooty **brushes her teeth** _____ .

   washes the floor   brushes her teeth

2. Rusty **jumps across the river** _____ .

   swims in the water   jumps across the river

3. Doogie **plays the drums** _____ .

   plays the drums   plays the flute

4. Rooty **falls asleep** _____ .

   reads a book   falls asleep

5. Doogie **dances fast** _____ .

   dances fast   sings loud

Activity Corner ▼▲▼▲▼▲▼▲▼▲▼▲▼▲▼

Pretend you are Rooty or Rusty. Write a letter to your grandfather about something funny that Doogie did. Use some exciting telling parts in your sentences.

Name

Sometimes the telling parts of two sentences can be joined. The word <u>and</u> is used to join the telling parts to make one sentence.

A. Look at the pictures. Join the telling parts of the two sentences to make one sentence. The first one has been done for you.

1. Kipper sits in the pouch. Kipper peeks out.

   Kipper sits in the pouch and peeks out.

2. This animal hops around. This animal plays.

   This animal hops around and plays.

3. Jacko lies down. Jacko falls asleep.

   Jacko lies down and falls asleep.

4. They have races. They hop fast.

   They have races and hop fast.

B. Join each pair of sentences. Use the word <u>and</u>. Write the new sentence. The first one has been done for you.

1. Koko sits in a tree. Koko eats leaves.

   Koko sits in a tree and eats leaves.

2. Her baby smiles. Her baby rides on her back.

   Her baby smiles and rides on her back.

3. Kipper looks up. Kipper sees the baby.

   Kipper looks up and sees the baby.

Harcourt Brace School Publishers

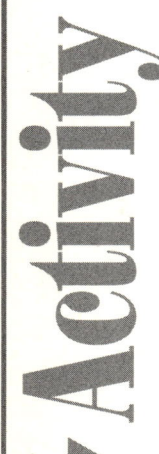

Activity Corner ▼▲▼▲▼▲▼▲▼▲▼

Pretend you are Kipper's friend. Tell Kipper how to play a game. Try to join some of the telling parts of your sentences with <u>and</u>.

WORD ORDER

Name

The words in a sentence are in an order that makes sense. If the words are mixed up, the sentence does not make sense.

A. Read each group of words. Circle the group of words if it makes sense. The first one has been done for you.

1. (Johnny Appleseed planted apple trees.)

2. ground in the seeds He put.

3. (He watered the trees.)

4. on were the trees Red apples.

5. (People ate the sweet apples.)

6. (He traveled to many places.)

7. was a pot His hat.

8. friends Johnny had many.

9. (Animals liked Johnny.)

10. fed Johnny animals.

B. Write each group of words in the correct order. The first one has been done for you.

1. pies Max makes.

   Max makes pies.

2. the apples He peels.

   He peels the apples.

3. helps Lara him.

   Lara helps him.

4. crust She rolls out the.

   She rolls out the crust.

5. the oven in bake The pies.

   The pies bake in the oven.

Corner

Activity

Make an apple mobile. You will need colored paper, scissors, yarn, and a pencil. First, cut out some apple shapes. On each one, write a sentence about how apples look, feel, and taste. Make sure your sentences make sense. Then cut pieces of yarn. Poke a hole through the top of each apple shape with your pencil. Tie a piece of yarn to each apple, and hang them in your classroom.

Name _____

A **statement** is a sentence that tells something. It begins with a capital letter. It ends with a **period (.)**.

A. Write each statement correctly. The first one has been done for you.

1. bert the bear was eight years old

   Bert the bear was eight years old.

2. his friends came to his party

   His friends came to his party.

3. they sang "Happy Birthday" to him

   They sang "Happy Birthday" to him.

4. there were a lot of candles on his cake

   There were a lot of candles on his cake.

5. he opened his gifts

   He opened his gifts.

6. the skates were great

   The skates were great.

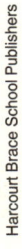

B. Read each sentence. Find the mistakes. Then write each statement correctly. The first one has been done for you.

1. a moose is Bert's best friend

   A moose is Bert's best friend.

2. they went ice skating together.

   They went ice skating together.

3. the ice was hard

   The ice was hard .

4. then Bert went across the pond.

   Then Bert went across the pond.

5. his skates slipped on the ice

   His skates slipped on the ice.

Harcourt Brace School Publishers

Activity Corner ▼▲▼▲▼▲▼▲▼▲▼▲▼

What other presents did Bert get for his birthday? Choose one to write clues about. Write three statements on the front of a sheet of paper. In each statement, tell a little about the present. On the back of the paper, draw what the present is. Trade papers with a classmate. Take turns reading each other's clues to guess the object.

Name _____

A **question** is a sentence that asks something. It ends with a **question mark (?)**.

A. Read each sentence. Write S for a sentence that is a statement. Write Q for a sentence that is a question. The first one has been done for you.

1. Do you want to join the circus? **Q** _____

2. My friend said it was great fun. **S** _____

3. What will you do? **Q** _____

4. I love to climb and swing. **S** _____

B. Write each sentence correctly. Be sure to use the correct end mark. The first one has been done for you.

1. why did you come to the circus

Why did you come to the circus? _____

2. can you do tricks

Can you do tricks?

3. do you want to see me fly

Do you want to see me fly?

4. how can monkeys fly

How can monkeys fly?

5. do you have a swing

Do you have a swing?

6. when can you start

When can you start?

Activity Corner ▽△▽△▽△▽△▽△▽△▽

Imagine that you are the monkey's friend at home. Write your friend a letter on another sheet of paper.

Ask her three questions about the circus.

SIDEWALKS SING – **Grammar Practice**

EXCLAMATIONS AND COMMANDS

Name _____

An **exclamation** is a sentence that shows strong feeling. It ends with an **exclamation point (!)**.

A **command** is a sentence that tells someone to do something. It ends with a **period (.)**.

A. Read each sentence. Circle E for exclamation if the sentence shows strong feeling. Circle C for command if the sentence tells someone to do something. The first one has been done for you.

1. Come downstairs to eat breakfast.   (C)   E

2. Today you will have a surprise!   C   (E)

3. I can't wait to find out what the surprise will be!   C   (E)

4. Eat your toast.   (C)   E

5. Put on your seat belt.   (C)   E

6. We'll be having fun very soon!   C   (E)

B. Write each sentence correctly. The first one has been done for you.

1. Wow, this is fun

   Wow, this is fun!

2. Don't run too fast

   Don't run too fast.

3. Listen to the happy music

   Listen to the happy music.

4. Hold on tight

   Hold on tight.

5. I am so scared

   I am so scared!

6. This was the best surprise ever

   This was the best surprise ever!

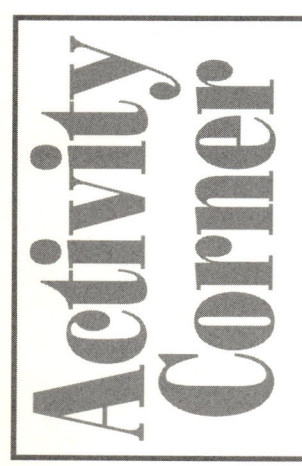

What is your favorite ride at an amusement park? Write a safety rule for that ride. Put a period at the end of your command. Then write an exclamation about an exciting ride. Use an exclamation point.

Name

A **statement** tells something.
It ends with a **period (.)**.

A **command** tells someone to do something.
It also ends with a **period (.)**.

A **question** asks something.
It ends with a **question mark (?)**.

An **exclamation** shows strong feeling.
It ends with an **exclamation point (!)**.

A. Read each sentence. Underline the end mark. Then darken the circle in front of the word that tells what kind of sentence it is. The first one has been done for you.

1. Do you want to run down the tree?
   ○ **statement**   ● **question**   ○ **command**

2. We will walk along the trail.
   ● **statement**   ○ **question**   ○ **exclamation**

3. What fun that will be!
   ○ **statement**   ○ **command**   ● **exclamation**

4. Chipmunks must be careful.
   ● **statement**   ○ **question**   ○ **exclamation**

5. Stay along the side of the path.
   ● **command**   ○ **question**   ○ **exclamation**

B. Read each sentence. Darken the circle in front of the correct end mark for the sentence. The first one has been done for you.

1. Are you tired ○ . ● ? ○ !

2. Hiking is hard work ● . ○ ? ○ !

3. Sit down and rest for a while ● . ○ ? ○ !

4. Can we find another way down ○ . ● ? ○ !

5. Wow, I've got a good idea ○ . ○ ? ● !

6. Follow me ● . ○ ? ○ !

7. Hooray for picnics ○ . ○ ? ● !

8. What yummy food this is ○ . ○ ? ● !

Activity Corner ▼▲▼▲▼▲▼▲▼▲▼▲▼▲▼

Write a story about the chipmunks at the picnic. Use another sheet of paper. Write three or four different kinds of sentences. Do not use end marks. Trade papers with a classmate. Add the correct end marks to each other's sentences.

NOUNS

Name

A word that names a person or an animal is called a **noun**.

A word that names a place or a thing is called a **noun**.

A. Underline the noun or nouns in each sentence. You should find eleven nouns in all. The first sentence has been done for you.

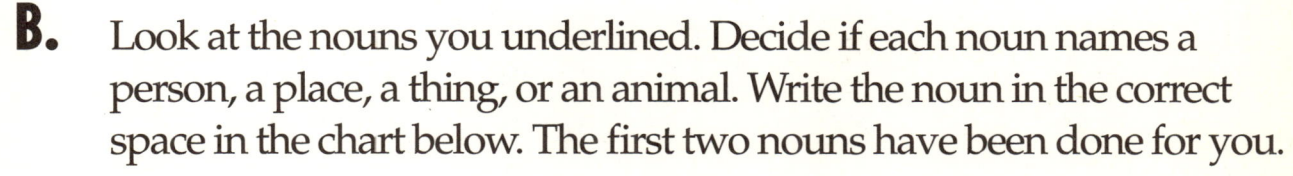

1. My <u>sister</u> plays in the <u>park</u>.
2. She rides in a <u>car</u> with our <u>mother</u>.
3. Sometimes our <u>dog</u> goes, too.
4. A <u>boy</u> feeds <u>birds</u> under the <u>trees</u>.
5. Let's go to the <u>playground</u>!
6. I see a <u>cat</u> under the <u>slide</u>.

B. Look at the nouns you underlined. Decide if each noun names a person, a place, a thing, or an animal. Write the noun in the correct space in the chart below. The first two nouns have been done for you.

Person	Place	Thing	Animal
sister	**park**	**car**	**dog**
mother	**playground**	**trees**	**birds**
boy		**slide**	**cat**

C. Choose nouns from the picture. Write them in the sentences. The first one has been done for you.

1. Here is the _____**market**_____ .

2. I like to make juice from _____**oranges**_____ .

3. Yellow _____**bananas**_____ are good in cereal.

4. There are red _____**tomatoes**_____ for a salad.

5. Green _____**beans**_____ are my favorite vegetable.

Activity Corner

On ten small pieces of paper, write nouns. Have a classmate choose one card at a time and tell you whether it is a person, animal, place, or thing.

SPECIAL NAMES AND TITLES OF PEOPLE

Name _____

Some nouns are the special names of people. These nouns are called proper nouns. Names of special people begin with **capital letters.**

Titles of people also begin with a capital letter. Most titles of people are followed by a **period (.).**

A. Write these special names and titles correctly. The first one has been done for you.

1. mr bobby walker

   Mr. Bobby Walker _____

2. mrs. hazel rivera

   Mrs. Hazel Rivera _____

3. dr max hobbs

   Dr. Max Hobbs _____

4. shayla jackson

   Shayla Jackson _____

5. ms rolanda choy

   Ms. Rolanda Choy _____

B. Write each sentence correctly. The first one has been done for you.

1. They invited gilbert to a party.

   They invited Gilbert to a party.

2. Did eddie start a pillow fight?

   Did Eddie start a pillow fight?

3. His dad, mr bellows, stopped it.

   His dad, Mr. Bellows, stopped it.

4. Then mrs bellows sent everyone to bed.

   Then Mrs. Bellows sent everyone to bed.

5. But gilbert couldn't sleep.

   But Gilbert couldn't sleep.

Activity Corner

Think about a time when you went to a party. Write about the party on another sheet of paper. Tell who was there and what they did. Be sure to include special names and titles.

NAMES OF SPECIAL ANIMALS AND PLACES

Name

Some **proper nouns** are the names of special animals. These names begin with a capital letter.

Some **proper nouns** are the names of special places. They also begin with a capital letter.

A. Look at the picture. Seven names of special animals and places are written incorrectly. Write them correctly on the lines below. The first one has been done for you.

1. **Annabelle**

2. **Brazil**

3. **Dallas**

4. **Omaha, Nebraska**

5. **Mr. Gobbles**

6. **South Street**

7. **Gruffy**

annabelle
brazil

Midnight
dallas, Texas

Nora and Katy
omaha, nebraska

mr. gobbles
south street

gruffy
Phoenix, Arizona

B. Read each sentence. Circle the name of the special animal or place that is written correctly. The first one has been done for you.

1. My dog (pete, (Pete)) is in trouble.

2. He went into ((Pine Woods), pine woods).

3. The people of ((Lakeside), lakeside) went to find him.

4. Then I saw them running down (main street, (Main Street)).

5. We named the skunk (smelly, (Smelly)).

6. We changed the name of the woods to ((Skunk Hollow), skunk hollow).

Activity Corner ▼▲▼▲▼▲▼▲▼▲▼▲▼▲▼

Pretend that you work in a pet shop. Make a list of pets that might be in the shop. Then make up a name for each pet. Write each name next to the pet in your list. Then write the street and city where your shop is.

NAMES OF DAYS AND MONTHS

Harcourt Brace School Publishers

Name

The names of days are **proper nouns**.
The names of days begin with a capital letter.

The names of months are **proper nouns**.
The names of months begin with a capital letter.

A. Write each sentence correctly. Add capital letters where they are needed. The first one has been done for you.

1. I started swimming lessons in june.

   I started swimming lessons in June.

2. On monday, I put my head under the water.

   On Monday, I put my head under the water.

3. I floated on wednesday.

   I floated on Wednesday.

4. By july, I was swimming.

   By July, I was swimming.

5. This friday, I am in a race.

   This Friday, I am in a race.

B. Write the name of a day or a month in each sentence. Be sure to use capital letters. The first blank has been filled in for you. **(Responses will vary.)**

1. On _____**Monday**_____, Maggie makes mudpies. **(day)**

2. On _____, Trudy twists taffy. **(day)**

3. Julie juggles jam jars in _____. **(month)**

4. Freddie flies the flag in _____. **(month)**

5. In _____, Nancy needs a notebook. **(month)**

6. On _____, Sally sews slippers. **(day)**

January March May July October November
February April June August September December

Monday • Tuesday • Wednesday • Thursday • Friday • Saturday • Sunday

Activity Corner ▼▲▼▲▼▲▼▲▼▲▼▲▼▲▼

Make a book of days. Write the name of each day of the week on a separate sheet of paper. Ask classmates to tell something they do on one of the days, and write what they do on that page. Put the pages together to make a book.

Name _____

The names of holidays are proper nouns. All important words in the names of holidays begin with capital letters.

A. Read each sentence. Circle the name of a holiday. Then write the name correctly. Use capital letters where they are needed. The first one has been done for you.

1. We plant a tree on (arbor day.)

   Arbor Day _____

2. We have a parade on the (fourth of july.)

   Fourth of July _____

3. We draw sailing ships on (columbus day.)

   Columbus Day _____

4. Red hearts cover the walls on (valentine's day.)

   Valentine's Day _____

5. I trick my mom on (april fool's day.)

   April Fool's Day _____

B. Read the list. Write the name of the holiday that you think of when you read each clue. The first one has been done for you.

1. turkey and stuffing   **Thanksgiving Day**

2. hearts   **Valentine's Day**

3. planting trees   **Arbor Day**

4. three sailing ships   **Columbus Day**

5. American flags and fireworks   **Fourth of July**

Activity Corner ▼▲▼▲▼▲▼▲▼▲▼▲▼

Plan a party for a make-believe holiday. Write an invitation for your party on a separate sheet of paper. Tell when the party is and where it will be. Make a menu of what you will serve at your party. Write a name for your holiday.

TITLES OF BOOKS

Name _____

The first word, the last word, and each important word in a book title begin with capital letters. The titles of books have a line under them.

A. Write each title correctly. Add capital letters where they are needed. Don't forget to draw a line under the titles! The first one has been done for you.

1. There are shiny colors in the rainbow fish.

   The Rainbow Fish
   _____

2. Lots of animals share a home in the mitten.

   The Mitten
   _____

3. A boy tells about his family in the stories julian tells.

   The Stories Julian Tells
   _____

4. Mama wants a coat in a new coat for anna.

   A New Coat for Anna
   _____

B. Read each clue. Then look at the story titles in the picture. Decide which one fits each clue. Write the title correctly on the line. The first one has been done for you.

1. A mother sends her son to the store for bacon.

   Don't Forget the Bacon

2. This book gives information about quicksand.

   The Quicksand Book

3. The story in this book happens at night.

   Night Noises

◢◣ Activity Corner ▼◤▼◢▼◤▼◢▼◤▼◢▼◤▼◢▼

Make a poster for a book you have read. Draw a picture from the story. Write the title and the author's name. Then write something about the book that would make others want to read it. Put the poster up in your classroom.

Name

Some nouns name more than one. Add the letter s to most nouns to name more than one.

A. Read each sentence. Make the underlined noun name more than one. Write the sentence. The first one has been done for you.

1. Mother sent me to get two jar of jam.

   Mother sent me to get two jars of jam.

2. Did she say two bag of ham?

   Did she say two bags of ham?

3. Did she say two leg of lamb?

   Did she say two legs of lamb?

4. At least I won't forget the parrot.

   At least I won't forget the parrots.

5. Did she say carrot?

   Did she say carrots?

B. Read the poster. Write the nouns that name more than one. The first one has been done for you.

YARD SALE TODAY!

1. Four soft pillows
2. Two tiny lamps
3. Hardly used skates
4. One coat with two buttons
5. Many mugs
6. Some good books

1. **pillows**
2. **lamps**
3. **skates**
4. **buttons**
5. **mugs**
6. **books**

Activity Corner

Plan a trip. Make a list of things you might take. Use some nouns that name more than one.

_____

_____

_____

PLURAL NOUNS WITH ES

Name _____

Some nouns end with es to name more than one. Words that end with s, x, ch, and sh add es to name more than one.

A. Read each sentence. Circle the correct noun. The first one has been done for you.

1. One day, a fisherman caught a large ((fish), fishes).

2. "This will make many good (lunch, (lunches)) for me," said the fisherman.

3. "If you let me go, I will give you three (wish, (wishes))," said the fish.

4. "Make these (box, (boxes)) into castles," the fisherman said.

5. In three (flash, (flashes)), there were three castles.

B. Read each sentence. Make the underlined noun name more than one. Write the new word. The first one has been done for you.

1. The fisherman asked for <u>bush</u> in front of the castles.

   bushes

2. Then he wanted <u>bench</u> near the bushes.

   benches

3. "I want <u>fox</u> in the fields," he said.

   foxes

4. "No," said the fish. "Your three <u>wish</u> are gone."

   wishes

5. It leaped in and out of the water with <u>splash</u> of joy.

   splashes

Harcourt Brace School Publishers

Activity Corner

Make up a fairy tale about someone who is granted three wishes. Use some nouns that end with <u>es</u> to name more than one. Draw pictures for your story. Share the story with your classmates.

OTHER PLURAL NOUNS

Name

Some nouns change spelling to name more than one.

A. Circle the noun that names more than one. Then write the sentence. The first one has been done for you.

1. The (child, (children)) learn to ski.

   The children learn to ski.

2. Warm boots are on their (foot, (feet)).

   Warm boots are on their feet.

3. Their (tooth, (teeth)) chatter from the cold.

   Their teeth chatter from the cold.

4. Those (man, (men)) are going to race.

   Those men are going to race.

5. The (woman, (women)) race, too.

   The women race, too.

B. Read each sentence. Change the word below the blank to make it name more than one. Write the word in the sentence. The first blank has been filled in for you.

1. Two ____**men**____ were the first to fly an airplane.
   man

2. It must have been a thrill when their ____**feet**____ left the ground.
   foot

3. Some early stunt pilots were ____**women**____ .
   woman

4. Today even some ____**children**____ fly planes.
   child

Harcourt Brace School Publishers

Activity Corner ▽▲▽▲▽▲▽▲▽▲▽▲▽

Have a plural race with a partner. On five slips of paper, write these words: <u>man</u>, <u>woman</u>, <u>child</u>, <u>tooth</u>, <u>foot</u>. Mix your words together with your partner's words. Turn the pile face down. Take turns picking a word from the pile. See how quickly you can say the plural of the word you pick.

Name

A pronoun is a word that takes the place of a noun. I, he, she, it, and they are pronouns. I tells about the speaker. He and she tell about other people. It tells about an animal or a thing. They tells about more than one.

A. Read the sentences. Circle the pronouns. The first one has been done for you.

1. (I) went to visit Grandma and Grandpa.

2. Grandma said (she) saw a deer.

3. Grandpa showed where (he) saw the deer.

4. (They) didn't know that (I) saw (it), too.

5. (I) saw a mother deer and a baby.

6. (They) were eating corn at night.

7. (It) grew behind my grandparents' house.

8. Grandma said (she) planted (it) for the deer.

B. Read each sentence. Use a pronoun for the underlined word or words. Write the new sentence. The first one has been done for you.

1. Rachel said, "<u>Rachel</u> will sing."

   Rachel said, "I will sing."

2. <u>Rachel</u> began to sing.

   She began to sing.

3. My baby brother heard <u>the sound</u>.

   My baby brother heard it.

4. <u>My baby brother</u> began to cry.

   He began to cry.

5. <u>Rachel and my baby brother</u> sang well together.

   They sang well together.

Activity Corner ▼▲▼▲▼▲▼▲▼▲▼▲▼▲▼

Write a story about something you like to do with friends. Or look at a story you have already written. Circle the pronouns <u>I</u>, <u>he</u>, <u>she</u>, <u>it</u>, and <u>they</u>. Is it clear who you mean when you use pronouns? Should you use more pronouns?

Harcourt Brace School Publishers

DESCRIBING WORDS

Name _____

A **describing word** tells about a noun.
Some describing words tell how something feels.

Some describing words tell how something tastes or smells.

Some describing words tell how something sounds.

A. Read the sentences. Circle the describing words. The first one has been done for you.

1. People may think that frogs have (bumpy) skin.

2. Really, they have (smooth) skin.

3. I like to listen to a (croaking) frog.

4. But you might not like its (swampy) smell!

5. Can you hear the (buzzing) bees?

6. Watch out for that (muddy) path!

B. Complete each sentence with a describing word from the box. The first blank has been filled in for you.
Responses may vary.

smoky	crunchy	fishy
sour	tasty	salty

1. This meat smells __smoky__ .

2. Would you like some __tasty__ chips?

3. When you bite that apple, it sounds __crunchy__ .

4. The tuna makes this salad taste __fishy__ .

5. Do you have some __sour__ candy in your backpack?

6. Please give me some of that __salty__ popcorn.

Activity Corner ▼▲▼▲▼▲▼▲▼▲▼

Write sentences that describe your favorite animal. Do not name the animal. Read your sentences to a classmate. Can your friend guess the animal? If not, use more describing words as clues.

Name _____

A **describing word** tells about a noun.
Some describing words tell about size, shape, or color.

Some describing words tell how many.

A. Read each sentence. Which word tells about the underlined word? Circle the describing word. The first one has been done for you.

1. An elephant has a (long) <u>trunk</u>.

2. It has a (round) <u>body</u>.

3. A mother elephant usually has (one) <u>baby</u>.

4. Sometimes a mother has (two) <u>babies</u>.

5. Then the <u>babies</u> are (small).

B. Read each sentence. Add a describing word. The first one has been done for you. **Responses will vary.**

1. A ___**white**___ bear walked on the snow.
   color

2. Soon ___**two**___ bear cubs followed her.
   how many

3. The mother bear took ___**giant**___ steps.
   size

4. The ___**little**___ bears could not keep up.
   size

5. They curled themselves into a ___**round**___ ball and slept.
   shape

Activity Corner ▼▲▼▲▼▲▼▲▼▲▼▲▼

Write a description of your pet or of a pet you would like to have. Does it have big, round eyes? Does it have two feet or four feet? Use words that describe. Then read your description to a partner. Have your partner draw a picture of the pet you described.

DESCRIBING WORDS THAT COMPARE

Name _____

A describing word that ends with <u>er</u> compares two things. A describing word that ends with <u>est</u> compares more than two things.

A. Add <u>er</u> or <u>est</u> to the word in parentheses to complete each sentence. Use the picture of the race to help you. The first one has been done for you.

1. Giraffe is the **tallest** runner. (tall)

2. Squirrel is **shorter** than Zebra. (short)

3. Giraffe has the **longest** neck. (long)

4. Zebra is **slower** than Squirrel. (slow)

5. Mouse is the **fastest** runner of all. (fast)

B. Add er and est to each word to complete
the chart. Some of the blanks have been
filled in for you.

1.	high	**higher**	**highest**
2.	small	**smaller**	**smallest**
3.	soft	**softer**	**softest**
4.	new	**newer**	**newest**
5.	loud	**louder**	**loudest**
6.	strong	**stronger**	**strongest**
7.	hard	**harder**	**hardest**
8.	old	**older**	**oldest**

Activity Corner ▽▲▽▲▽▲▽▲▽▲▽▲▽

Choose three places, animals, or things. Write sentences
that tell how they are different. Use describing words with
er and est. Draw a picture to go with each sentence.

Name _____

An **action verb** is a word that tells what someone or something does.

A verb can tell about an action that happens now. Add <u>s</u> to an action verb that tells what one person, animal, or thing does.

A. Add <u>s</u> to each verb to make a new word. The first one has been done for you.

1. wear   **wears** _____

2. play   **plays** _____

3. pretend   **pretends** _____

4. turn   **turns** _____

5. pull   **pulls** _____

6. cheer   **cheers** _____

B. Write a word from the box to complete each sentence. The first one has been done for you.

wears	turns	pretend
play	cheer	pulls

1. Alicia and Tim __**play**__ the queen and the king in our school play.

2. Alicia __**wears**__ a big, shiny crown on her head.

3. Alf __**pulls**__ the curtain and the play begins.

4. The children __**pretend**__ they live far away.

5. The wicked king __**turns**__ into a frog.

6. People __**cheer**__ when the play is over.

Activity Corner

Begin a chart of interesting action words. Make two lists on the chart. Write <u>one</u> at the top of the first list. Write <u>more than one</u> at the top of the second list. Put the chart in your desk. Then add to the chart any action words you know. Add to the chart any time you hear or read an interesting action word. Remember to use some of the words in your own writing.

Name _____

A verb can tell about an action that happened in the past. Many verbs end with ed to tell about something that happened in the past.

A. Add ed to each word to make it tell about the past. The first one has been done for you.

1. dream   **dreamed** _____

2. water   **watered** _____

3. look   **looked** _____

4. plant   **planted** _____

5. paint   **painted** _____

6. count   **counted** _____

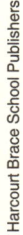

Harcourt Brace School Publishers

B. Choose one of the words from the box to complete each sentence. The first one has been done for you.

| painted | looked | counted |
| dreamed | planted | watered |

1. Jack __**planted**__ five sunflower seeds.

2. He __**painted**__ a sign that said "DO NOT TOUCH."

3. Jack __**watered**__ the plants so they would grow.

4. He __**looked**__ at them through a hand lens.

5. He __**counted**__ how many flowers bloomed.

6. Jack __**dreamed**__ that one flower grew very tall.

Activity Corner ▽▲▽▲▽▲▽▲▽▲▽▲▽

Look through some books. Make a list of six action words that end in ed. Then work with a partner to make up a story. Use some or all of the words.

_____   _____

_____   _____

_____   _____

Name _____

Some verbs do not show action. They tell what someone or something is like. The verbs is, are, and am tell about now.

Use is to tell about one person, place, animal, or thing. Use are to tell about more than one. Use am with the word I.

A. Write is, are, or am to complete each sentence. The first one has been done for you.

1. A rain shower _____**is**_____ very colorful.

2. The sun _____**is**_____ bright yellow.

3. Clouds _____**are**_____ gray and white.

4. The rainbow _____**is**_____ beautiful.

5. My umbrella _____**is**_____ green, blue, and purple.

6. The raindrops _____**are**_____ shiny and clear.

7. Puddles _____**are**_____ fun to splash in.

8. I _____**am**_____ wet!

B. Circle the correct verb. Then complete the sentence in your own words. Write the sentence. The first one has been done for you.

Responses will vary.

1. The flowers (is, (are)) _____.

   The flowers are yellow and red. _____

2. The sky ((is,) are) _____.

   _____

3. The grass ((is,) are) _____.

   _____

Corner ▼▲▼▲▼▲▼▲▼▲▼▲▼▲▼

On another sheet of paper, write sentences that describe you and a classmate. How tall are you? What are you wearing? Then write sentences that tell how the two of you are alike and how you are different. Share your sentences with another classmate.

Name _____

The verbs <u>was</u> and <u>were</u> tell about the past. Use <u>was</u> to tell about one person, place, animal, or thing. Use <u>were</u> to tell about more than one.

A. Write <u>was</u> or <u>were</u> to complete each sentence. The first one has been done for you.

1. My trip to Africa _____**was**_____ an adventure.

2. Every day _____**was**_____ different.

3. A lioness and her cubs _____**were**_____ asleep.

4. Monkeys _____**were**_____ high in the trees.

5. A singing bird _____**was**_____ brightly colored.

6. Four zebras _____**were**_____ in the grass.

7. Our jeep _____**was**_____ very old.

8. Its seats _____**were**_____ lumpy.

B. Choose the correct verb. Write the sentence. The first one has been done for you.

1. The sun ((was), were) hot.

   The sun was hot.

2. Some animals (was, (were)) in the water.

   Some animals were in the water.

3. Two giraffes (was, (were)) hungry.

   Two giraffes were hungry.

4. An elephant ((was), were) with its baby.

   An elephant was with its baby.

Activity Corner

Make a photograph album of a trip to an animal park or a zoo. Choose from pages 65 and 66 five sentences that tell about animals. Write each sentence on a sheet of drawing paper. Then draw a picture to go with the sentence. Make a booklet with the pages. You may want to make a cover for your album too.

HAS, HAVE, HAD

Name _____

The verbs has and have tell about now. The verb had tells about the past. Use has to tell about one person or thing. Use have to tell about more than one.

A. Write has, have, or had to complete each sentence. The first one has been done for you.

1. Last week, Katie _____**had**_____ one dog named Pepper.

2. Then Pepper _____**had**_____ four puppies.

3. Now Katie _____**has**_____ five pets to take care of!

4. One puppy _____**has**_____ brown spots.

5. Two puppies _____**have**_____ white spots.

6. The smallest puppy _____**has**_____ one black spot around its eye.

B. Find the mistake in each sentence. First, circle the verb _has_, _have_, or _had_. Then, rewrite the sentence, using the correct verb. The first one has been done for you.

1. Katie (have) fun with the puppies.

   Katie has fun with the puppies.

2. They all (has) black, wet noses.

   They all have black, wet noses.

3. Yesterday one puppy (has) a sock.

   Yesterday one puppy had a sock.

4. Today he (have) a toy to play with.

   Today he has a toy to play with.

Corner ▽▲▽▲▽▲▽▲▽▲▽▲▽▲▽

With a partner, write a story about animal babies. Choose an animal that lives in the wild or one that you could have as a pet. First, list everything you know about the animal. Then, write your story. Use _has_, _have_, and _had_ in some of your sentences.

Name _____

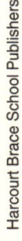

A helping verb works with the verb to show action. Use <u>has</u>, <u>have</u>, and <u>had</u> with other verbs to show action that happened in the past. Use <u>has</u> to tell what one person, animal, or thing did. Use <u>have</u> to tell what more than one person, animal, or thing did.

A. Choose the correct helping verb. Write it in the sentence. The first one has been done for you.

1. Our family _____**has**_____ (have, has) always wanted a cat.

2. A little kitten _____**had**_____ (have, had) crawled under our porch.

3. Soon we _____**had**_____ (has, had) decided to let her in.

4. She _____**has**_____ (have, has) lived with us ever since.

5. We _____**have**_____ (have, has) named her Trouble. Guess why!

B. Use <u>has</u>, <u>have</u>, or <u>had</u> to complete each sentence. Write the sentence. The first one has been done for you.

1. The vase _____ fallen on the floor.

   The vase has fallen on the floor.

2. Who _____ broken it?

   Who has/had broken it?

3. Tisha and Andy _____ found clues.

   Tisha and Andy have found clues.

4. That cat _____ done it again!

   That cat has/had done it again!

Activity Corner

Imagine that you got a wonderful new pet last week. Write a story about something you and your pet have done together. Be sure to use the helping verbs <u>have</u>, <u>has</u>, and <u>had</u> in your story.

SEE AND GIVE

Name _____

The verbs <u>see</u> and <u>give</u> tell about now. Add <u>s</u> to tell what one person, animal, or thing sees or gives.

The verbs <u>saw</u> and <u>gave</u> tell about the past. These action verbs do not add <u>ed</u> to tell about the past.

A. Choose the correct verb to complete the sentence. The first one has been done for you.

1. Once a year the children _____**see**_____ (see, sees) a museum show.

2. The teacher _____**gives**_____ (give, gives) everyone a ticket.

3. At the door, Pat _____**gives**_____ (give, gives) the person her ticket.

4. We _____**see**_____ (see, sees) the dinosaurs first.

5. Their huge bones _____**give**_____ (give, gives) me chills.

6. My friend _____**sees**_____ (see, sees) that I'm not really scared.

B. Write the sentences in a paragraph. Change <u>see</u> and <u>give</u> to make them tell about the past. The first sentence has been done for you.

1. At the museum store I see something to buy.
2. I give some money to a woman.
3. My friends see my new toy dinosaur!
4. I give John a turn to play with it.

At the museum store I saw something to buy. I gave some money to a woman. My friends saw my new toy dinosaur! I gave John a turn to play with it.

Harcourt Brace School Publishers

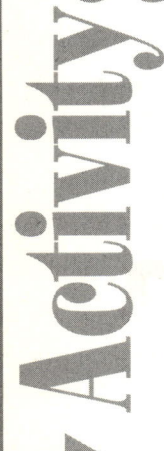

Activity Corner ▼▲▼▲▼▲▼▲▼▲▼▲▼

Tell a partner about something you can see from your chair. It should be something that is happening now. Have your partner raise his or her hand whenever you say the word <u>see</u>. Then it's your partner's turn to tell about something he or she saw yesterday. Raise your hand whenever your partner says the word <u>saw</u>. Play the game again with the words <u>give</u> and <u>gave</u>.

Name _____

The verbs come and run tell about now.
Add s to tell what one person, animal, or
thing does.

The verbs came and ran tell about the past.

A. Choose the correct verb to complete
the sentence. The first one has been
done for you.

1. A tortoise _____**comes**_____ (come, comes) down the path.

2. The tortoise and a hare _____**run**_____ (run, runs) into each other.

3. "A hare _____**runs**_____ (run, runs) very fast," says the hare.

4. "No other animal _____**comes**_____ (come, comes) close to me!"

5. "No tortoise _____**runs**_____ (run, runs) at all," he says.

6. The two animals _____**come**_____ (come, comes) out from the forest.

B. Write the sentences in a paragraph. Change <u>come</u> and <u>run</u> to make them tell about the past. The first sentence has been done for you.

1. The tortoise and the hare come to the starting line.
2. The hare quickly runs out of sight.
3. The tortoise comes along slowly.
4. It comes to the finish line first.

The tortoise and the hare came to the starting line. The hare quickly ran out of sight. The tortoise came along slowly. It came to the finish line first.

Activity Corner

Make up some sentences that use the words <u>come</u>, <u>comes</u>, <u>run</u>, <u>runs</u>, <u>came</u>, and <u>ran</u>, such as Dewayne <u>runs slowly</u> or I <u>came through the door</u>. Take turns with a partner acting out each other's sentences.

Name _____

The verbs go and do tell about now. Add es to tell what one person, animal, or thing does.

To tell about the past, the spelling of these verbs changes to went and did.

A. Choose the correct verb to complete the sentence. The first one has been done for you.

1. We ____**go**____ (go, goes) to school every weekday.

2. All over the country, other children ____**do**____ (do, does) this too.

3. The school bus ____**goes**____ (go, goes) right by my house.

4. My brother ____**does**____ (do, does) the same thing every morning.

5. He ____**goes**____ (go, goes) right to the computer room before class.

6. The computers ____**do**____ (do, does) a lot of work for him.

B. Change the verb to make each sentence tell about the past. Write the sentence. The first one has been done for you.

1. Long ago, children (go) to school less often.

   Long ago, children went to school less often.

2. Instead, they (do) work at home.

   Instead, they did work at home.

3. My great-grandmother (go) to school on horseback.

   My great-grandmother went to school on horseback.

   _____

4. She (go) even in snow or rain.

   She went even in snow or rain.

Activity Corner ▼▲▼▲▼▲▼▲▼▲▼▲▼

Make a chart to compare school today with school long ago. On one side, list things you do in school, for example, I do my writing on a computer. On the other side, list ways school was different long ago.

AGREEMENT

Name _____

When the naming part of a sentence tells about one person or thing, the verb ends in s. When a naming part tells about more than one, the verb does not end in s.

A. Choose the correct verb. Write it in the sentence. The first one has been done for you.

1. Some dogs _____**live**_____ (live, lives) in our homes as pets.

2. Other dogs _____**work**_____ (work, works) hard for us.

3. Some dogs _____**help**_____ (help, helps) people that cannot see.

4. One German shepherd _____**sniffs**_____ (sniff, sniffs) out drugs for the police.

5. A trained dog _____**acts**_____ (act, acts) in movies and television.

6. Sheepdogs _____**herd**_____ (herd, herds) flocks of sheep.

B. Choose the correct verb to complete each sentence. Write the sentences in a paragraph. Then add more sentences of your own. The first sentence has been done for you. **Additional sentences will vary.**

1. Some dogs (help, helps) people.
2. Most of us (know, knows) about guide dogs.
3. Dogs (help, helps) people who are deaf, too.
4. The dog (hear, hears) the doorbell ring.

Some dogs help people. **Most of us know about guide dogs. Dogs help people who are deaf, too. The dog hears the doorbell ring. Then it runs to its owner. A dog often picks up things for its owner.**

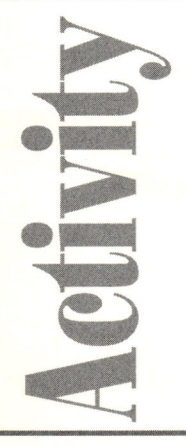

Activity Corner • • • • • • • • • • •

On another sheet of paper, write a story about a dog with a job. Ask a classmate to check your story to make sure the verbs agree with the naming parts. Then draw a picture of the dog at work.

Name

A **contraction** is a short way to write two words. When a contraction is made, one or more letters are left out. An **apostrophe (')** takes the place of the missing letter or letters.

A. Read each sentence. Write the contraction for the underlined words. The first one has been done for you.

1. We have gone to the park every summer.   **We've**

2. But I have not yet ridden the roller coaster.   **haven't**

3. This year I did not want to miss the fun.   **didn't**

4. Dad said, "Do not be scared."   **Don't**

5. "It will be over quickly."   **It'll**

6. "And you will have fun!"   **you'll**

Harcourt Brace School Publishers

B. Read each sentence. Underline the contraction. Then write the two words that make up the contraction. The first one has been done for you.

1. "All right, I'll do it," I said. **I will**

2. I hope I'm not scared, I thought. **I am**

3. It's very high at the top of that hill. **It is**

4. But there wasn't even time to yell. **was not**

5. I don't believe how fast we went! **do not**

6. They said they're riding it again. **they are**

Harcourt Brace School Publishers

Activity Corner ▽▲▽▲▽▲▽▲▽▲▽▲▽▲▽

Tell a story to a partner about an adventure of your own. Your partner should listen for contractions as you talk and clap softly whenever he or she hears one. Then listen and clap while your partner tells you a story.